# MANUFACTURING

## Exploring Career Pathways

*Diane Lindsey Reeves*

Created and produced by
Bright Futures Press, Cary, North Carolina
www.brightfuturespress.com

Published by
Cherry Lake Publishing, Ann Arbor, Michigan
www.cherrylakepublishing.com

Photo Credits: Cover, Beautyline; page 7,8, Phovoir; page 7, 10, FERNANDO BLANCO CALZADA; page 7, 12, Phovoir; page 7, 14, Mikko Lemola; page 7, 16, Stock-Asso; page 7, 18, imredesiuk; page 7, 20, Kzenon; page 7, 22, sciencephoto; page 24, Guo Zhong Hua.

Library of Congress Cataloging-in-Publication Data

Names: Reeves, Diane Lindsey, 1959- author.
Title: Manufacturing / Diane Lindsey Reeves.
Description: Ann Arbor, Michigan : Cherry Lake Publishing, [2017] I Series:
    World of work I Audience: Grades 4 to 6. I Includes bibliographical
    references and index.
Identifiers: LCCN 2016042183I ISBN 9781634726276 (hardcover) I ISBN
    9781634726474 (pbk.) I ISBN 9781634726375 (pdf) I ISBN 9781634726573
    (ebook)
Subjects: LCSH: Industrialists--Juvenile literature. I Manufacturing
    industries--Vocational guidance--Juvenile literature. I
    Occupations--Juvenile literature. I CYAC: Vocational guidance.
Classification: LCC HD9720.5 .R47 2017 I DDC 670.92--dc23
LC record available at https://lccn.loc.gov/2016042183

Printed in the United States of America.

# TABLE OF CONTENTS

# HELLO WORLD OF WORK

## This is you.

Right now, your job is to go to school and learn all you can.

## This is the world of work.

It's where people earn a living, find purpose in their lives, and make the world a better place.

Sooner or later, you'll have to find your way from

**HERE** to **THERE.**

To get started, take all the jobs in the incredibly enormous world of work and organize them into an imaginary pile. It's a big pile, isn't it? It would be pretty tricky to find the perfect job for you among so many options.

# No worries!

Some very smart career experts have made it easier to figure out. They sorted jobs and industries into groups by the types of skills and products they share. These groups are called career clusters. They provide pathways that will make it easier for you to find career options that match your interests.

- Architecture & Construction
- Arts & Communications
- Business & Administration
- Education & Training
- Finance
- Food & Natural Resources
- Government
- Health Sciences
- Hospitality & Tourism
- Human Services
- Information Technology
- Law & Public Safety
- Manufacturing
- Marketing
- Science, Technology, Engineering & Mathematics (STEM)
- Transportation

# Good thing you are still a kid.

You have lots of time to explore ideas and imagine yourself doing all kinds of amazing things. The **World of Work** (WoW for short) series of books will help you get started.

# TAKE A HIKE!

There are 16 career pathways waiting for you to explore. The only question is: Which one should you explore first?

Is **Manufacturing** a good path for you to start exploring career ideas? There is a lot to like about this pathway. These professionals make everything you could possibly imagine—from rocket ships to rubber bands. They even make, maintain, and repair the machines to make these things. Modern manufacturing has gone high-tech and offers many challenging, high-paying opportunities.

See if any of the following questions grab your interest.

**WOULD YOU ENJOY** figuring out how things are made, competing in a robot-building contest, or putting model airplanes together?

**CAN YOU IMAGINE** someday working at a high-tech manufacturing plant, engineering firm, or global logistics company?

**ARE YOU CURIOUS ABOUT** what chemical engineers, industrial designers, supply chain managers, robotics technologists, or welders do?

If so, it's time to take a hike! Keep reading to see what kinds of opportunities you can discover along the Manufacturing pathway.

## But wait!

What if you don't think you'll like this pathway?

You have two choices.

You could keep reading, to find out more than you already know. You might be surprised to learn how many amazing careers you'll find along this path.

OR

Turn to page 27 to get ideas about other WoW pathways.

**ENVIRONMENTAL SOLUTIONS DIRECTOR**

**ROBOTICS ENGINEER**

**PRODUCTION MANAGER**

**A&P TECHNICIAN**

# WoW Up Close

They design products. They operate complicated manufacturing equipment. They keep factories environmentally friendly and safe. These are just some of the important jobs that people who work along the Manufacturing pathway do.

**INDUSTRIAL DESIGNER**

**NANOTECHNOLOGIST**

**ELECTRICAL ENGINEER**

**CAM PROGRAMMER**

# A&P TECHNICIAN

**Airframe and powerplant (A&P)** technician is the official title of a certified aviation mechanic. These highly trained professionals keep the world flying high by working on everything from hot air balloons to jet engines. A&P technicians repair problems and prevent them from happening with inspections and maintenance.

You may have seen an aviation mechanic in action while waiting to board an airplane for a trip. As soon as an airplane lands at an airport, aircraft mechanics must perform a careful inspection of all systems before the airplane is cleared to take off again. This isn't just a simple matter of checking the oil and seeing if the tires are going flat. Jet engines have millions of parts. Jets that need repairs or maintenance are taken to huge **hangars** equipped with special tools.

There is a lot to know when it comes to keeping jet engines in top flying condition. Jets have two main areas. One is the powerplant, which is the engine. The other is the airframe. That includes the **fuselage**, the supporting frame and skin, and the doors, windows, and wings. Some mechanics specialize in one area or the other. A&P mechanics can do both. These highly trained mechanics keep bad things from happening when any of these vital parts malfunction.

## Check It Out!

Find out how jet engines work at

▶ http://bit.ly/BuildJet

▶ http://bit.ly/JetWorks

## Start Now!

✔ Keep your eyes on the sky and see if you can identify the different types of jets flying around up there.

✔ Volunteer to help your parent change the oil or fix a flat tire on the family's car.

✔ Have fun figuring out how airplanes fly by engineering your own paper airplanes at http://www.foldnfly.com.

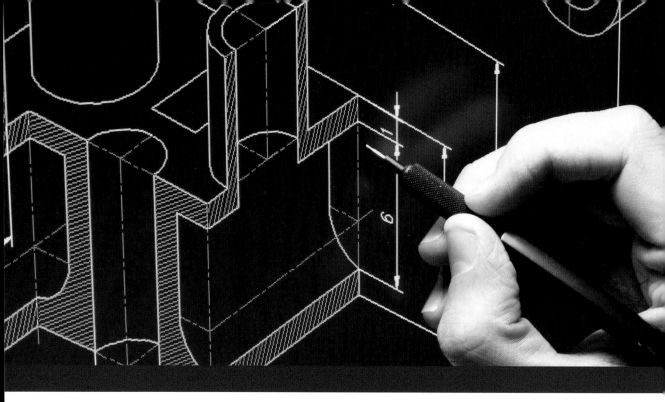

# CAM PROGRAMMER

Manufacturing involves making enormous amounts of the same product. Making lots of anything—whether it's blue jeans or automobiles—requires doing the same things over and over again. Many of these tasks would be difficult, dangerous, or, to be quite honest, downright boring for humans to do. That's why manufacturing uses machines to **automate** many processes.

Unlike humans, machines can't figure out what they are supposed to do. That's where **computer-aided manufacturing (CAM) programmers** come in. The machines used to make products are controlled by computers. These computers are controlled by humans. CAM programmers use special software to program machines to do very specific tasks.

It usually takes several different machines to make a single product. Take candy bars, for instance. One machine mixes the ingredients, while another one pours the mixed ingredients into molds. The candy bars must be wrapped and packaged for shipping. Everything must be done in a precise order with absolute accuracy. Otherwise, chocolate covered catastrophes can happen!

So, yes, in case you are wondering, CAM programmers must be tech-savvy and good at math.

## Check It Out!

Go online to find factories in your home state at

▶ http://factorytoursusa.com

Talk to a parent or teacher about arranging a tour of a nearby factory to see for yourself how stuff is made.

## Start Now!

Use online and library resources to find answers to questions like:

- ✓ Play around with computer science at https://studio. code.org.

- ✓ Use the Internet and library resources to find out how some of your favorite products are made. Pay special attention to how machines are used to make them.

# ELECTRICAL ENGINEER

What do a tiny microchip in your smartphone and
a giant generator that powers an entire city have in
common? They both need electricity to work!

**Electrical engineers** are plugged into anything and everything that uses electricity. That includes your favorite high-tech gadgets and the machines that make those computers, smartphones, and video game consoles. It includes the power plants that light your home and the world around you.

You'll find electrical engineers working in all kinds of places. They are involved in one way or another in making just about any product you can imagine. They design power systems for everything from rocket ships to radios. They develop new and better products and test electrical systems. They work in the military, in mines, in power plants, and in all kinds of manufacturing companies.

Would you like to know more about power systems and energy conversion, semiconductor devices and circuits, and electromagnetic fields and waves? Those are just some of the things you'll learn about if you go to college to become an electrical engineer. Electrical engineering is one way to put a spark into your future career!

## Check It Out!

Find out more about electricity at

▶ http://bit.ly/NyeElectric

▶ http://bit.ly/HowElectricity

▶ http://bit.ly/BrainPopElectric

## Start Now!

☑ Use the Internet and library resources to find out more about the "history of electricity."

☑ Electrify your next science fair project. Find ideas online at Web sites like http://bit.ly/ElectSci.

☑ Make a list of all the ways you use electricity at home and at school.

# ENVIRONMENTAL SOLUTIONS DIRECTOR

Manufacturing sometimes gets messy. There can be toxic chemicals involved. Or wastewater and other materials. Even air pollution. Those things aren't good for the environment. Fortunately, many manufacturers are finding smarter, **sustainable** ways to make products *and* protect the earth.

It is up to **environmental solutions directors** to help manufacturers go green. Environmental solutions directors start by looking carefully at what their company does and how they do it. Their first responsibility is to make sure that the company is obeying environmental safety laws. These can be strict and involve things like air quality, waste, clean water, and pollution.

From there, environmental solutions directors look at better ways for companies to do what they do. Is the company using too much energy? They find ways to be more energy efficient. Is the company producing too much waste? They might start a recycling program or look at ways to reuse waste products. Biodiesel fuel is one example of how this works. The fuel is made from oil that fast-food restaurants used to fry french fries. It's a story of how one company's trash becomes another company's treasure.

Besides the benefits of a cleaner, safer world, many manufacturers find that going green results in better product quality and smoother manufacturing processes. Yay for green manufacturing!

## Check It Out!

Play around with going green at

- https://www.earthrangers.com
- https://www3.epa.gov/recyclecity
- http://meetthegreens.pbskids.org/games

## Start Now!

- ✓ Measure your carbon footprint at http://bit.ly/GreenFoot.
- ✓ Get involved in your school's recycling program.
- ✓ Check the local news to see how local factories are addressing environmental problems.

# INDUSTRIAL DESIGNER

Cars, home appliances, toys, and other cool products don't just happen. They all start with an idea in the mind of an **industrial designer**. Industrial designers use a combination of art, business, and engineering skills to make products that people use every day.

There are lots of things to consider when designing a new product. How will the product be used? What does the product look like? What are the best materials to use in making it? How much will it cost to make it? Industrial designers use the answers to questions like these to create functional, attractive products that people can afford to buy.

Industrial designers use computers and computer-aided design (CAD) software to sketch out their ideas. Three-dimensional printers allow them to make samples of their products. These are called prototypes, and they are used to test products before they are manufactured.

Industrial designers tend to specialize in certain types of products. Some design sports equipment, while others design computers and smartphones. Still others work on medical equipment, furniture, or packaging.

A college degree in industrial design, architecture, or engineering is required to get a job like this. A **portfolio** filled with examples of their best design ideas help industrial designers land jobs and find new clients.

# Check It Out!

Find out more about industrial design at

- http://bit.ly/IndustDesign
- http://bit.ly/DeltaArt
- http://bit.ly/IndusDay

# Start Now!

- ✔ Create an idea book to make sketches of things you see in nature, stores, or anywhere.
- ✔ Take an after-school art class.
- ✔ Make a list of cool products you like to use.

# NANOTECHNOLOGIST

Here's a riddle for you. It is one of the biggest surprises in science, yet it's so small you can't touch it or even see it with a light microscope. What is it?

**Nanotechnology!**

**Nanotechnologists** are scientists and engineers who work with some of the world's smallest particles to create new and better products. These particles are so small they are measured in **nanometers**. How small is a nanometer? Look at the lead in your pencil. Its diameter is about a millimeter. One million nanometers could fit on the tip of your pencil.

Nanotechnologists are part researcher and part inventor. They work with nano-sized materials to create new products molecule by molecule. Their work requires high-tech scientific equipment, computers, and very powerful microscopes.

Nanotechnology is big news in manufacturing because better products can often be made with cleaner energy sources and at a lower cost. So far, nanotechnology is being used in everything from golf clubs and tennis balls to TV screens and computers. More effective medicines are being made and so are stain-resistant fabrics.

## Check It Out!

Go online to explore nanotechnology at

 http://www.nanooze.org

http://www.nanozone.org

## Start Now!

- ✔ Use the Internet to find information about "nanotechnology innovations." Make a list of the coolest ideas you find.

- ✔ Figure out how tall you are in nanometers.

# PRODUCTION MANAGER

Visit any manufacturing factory and it won't take long to see that it is a very busy place. There are lots of people. Lots of raw materials. Lots of complicated machines. You may even find some very busy robots.

Someone has to make sure that all these people, materials, and machines are doing what they need to do to get the job done. That someone is a **production manager**. Production managers are manufacturing experts. They know what is being made, how to make it, and who does each job. They are in charge of keeping the workplace safe and producing quality products. They make schedules and order materials. They train employees and prepare reports.

Boring is not a word you'd use to describe this job. It involves variety and responsibility. Good people skills are a must. The best production managers are well organized, strong leaders, and good communicators. They bring out the best in their employees and somehow make it all look easy.

It is up to production managers to make sure that the right amount of high-quality products is made on time and on budget. No pressure, right?

## Check It Out!

Ever wonder how your favorite products get made? Go online to the Science Channel and find out at

▶ http://www.sciencechannel.com/tv-shows/how-its-made

## Start Now!

✓ Create a master calendar to organize your family's activities and chores.

✓ Volunteer to help out at your school's fun run, field day, or another big event.

✓ Get involved in your school's peer mediation program.

# ROBOTICS ENGINEER

What if there was a robot that could clean your room and drive you to school? Hard as it may be to believe, there already are robots that can do those things! Robots drive cars, vacuum floors, and much, much more.

All these advances are made possible by **robotics engineers**. They design, make, and operate robots that do the things people either can't or don't want to do. Robots are used in manufacturing to make jobs safer, easier, and more efficient.

Building robots takes lots of time, talent, and technical skill. Robotics engineers start the process with research. They figure out what a robot needs to do and the best way to do it. They use a mix of mechanical, manufacturing, and electrical engineering know-how to design and test robots.

Robotics engineers design a robot's "body" and also its "brain." Robots may do humanlike things, but they cannot think. Robots can't do anything until a robotics engineer programs them to do very specific tasks.

It's a complicated process, but the results are worth the effort. A well-designed robot can get the job done. It can work 24/7 with no sick days, no excuses, and no drama!

# Check It Out!

Find out more about how robots work at

▶ http://science. howstuffworks.com/robot1. htm

▶ http://bit.ly/NatGeoRobot

▶ http://bit.ly/RobotHow

# Start Now!

✓ Make a list of ways robots could make your everyday life easier.

✓ Save up some money to buy a kit to make your very own robot.

Air-conditioning technician • Aircraft structure and systems assembler • **AIRFRAME AND POWERPLANT (A&P) TECHNICIAN** • Apparel patternmaker • Appliance mechanic • Application software developer • Assembler • Automatic teller machine technician • Auto mechanic • Baker • Biofuels process technician • Biological technician • Boilermaker • Cabinetmaker • Chemical operator • Chemical plant supervisor • Civil engineer • Computer-aided design programmer • **COMPUTER-AIDED MANUFACTURING (CAM) PROGRAMMER** • Drill operator • **ELECTRICAL ENGINEER** • Electromechanical equipment assembler •

# WoW Big List

Take a look at some of the different kinds of jobs people do in the Manufacturing pathway. **WoW!**

Some of these job titles will be familiar to you. Others will be so unfamiliar that you will scratch your head and say "huh?"

Electronics assembler • Electronic data processing auditor • Electronics engineer • Elevator installer • Engine builder • Engraver • Environmental engineer • Environmental health specialist • **ENVIRONMENTAL SOLUTIONS DIRECTOR** • Escalator service technician • Fabricator • Fabric cutter • Finisher • Fuel cell technician • Geothermal technician • Gluing pressman • Hazardous materials technician • Heavy equipment mechanic • **INDUSTRIAL DESIGNER** • Industrial engineer • Industrial hygienist • Industrial production manager • Jeweler • Laboratory technician • Locksmith • Machine operator • Machinist • Manufacturing engineer • Manufacturing production technician • Mechanical engineer • Medical appliance technician • Metal caster • Milling machine operator • Millwright • Model maker • **NANOTECHNOLOGIST** • Nuclear engineer • Operations manager • Packaging machine operator • Photonics technician • Photo technologist • Planing machine operator • Power plant supervisor • Process engineer • Product designer • **PRODUCTION MANAGER** •

Find a job title that makes you curious. Type the name of the job into your favorite Internet search engine and find out more about the people who have that job.

 What do they do?

 Where do they work?

How much training do they need to do this job?

Production worker • Punch press operator • Purchasing agent • Quality assurance inspector • Radiation control technician • Repair technician • Researcher • **ROBOTICS ENGINEER** • Robotics technician • Roustabout • Seamstress • Semiconductor processor • Sheet metal technician • Solar thermal technician • Supervisor • Tool and die maker • Upholsterer • Water quality analyst • Weatherization installer • Welder • Winder operator

# TAKE YOUR PICK

| | Put stars next to your 3 favorite career ideas | Put an X next to the career idea you like the least | Put a question mark next to the career idea you want to learn more about |
|---|---|---|---|
| A&P Technician | | | |
| CAM Programmer | | | |
| Electrical Engineer | | | |
| Environmental Solutions Director | | | |
| Industrial Designer | | | |
| Nanotechnologist | | | |
| Production Manager | | | |
| Robotics Engineer | | | |
| | What do you like most about these careers? | What is it about this career that doesn't appeal to you? | What do you want to learn about this career? Where can you find answers? |
| | | | |

Which Big Wow List ideas are you curious about?

# EXPLORE SOME MORE

The Manufacturing pathway is only one of 16 career pathways that hold exciting options for your future. Take a look at the other 15 to figure out where to start exploring next.

 ## Architecture and Construction

**WOULD YOU ENJOY** making things with LEGOs™, building a treehouse or birdhouse, or designing the world's best skate park?

**CAN YOU IMAGINE** someday working at a construction site, a design firm, or a building company?

**ARE YOU CURIOUS ABOUT** what civil engineers, demolition technicians, heavy-equipment operators, landscape architects, or urban planners do?

 ## Arts & Communications

**WOULD YOU ENJOY** drawing your own cartoons, using your smartphone to make a movie, or writing articles for the student newspaper?

**CAN YOU IMAGINE** someday working at a Hollywood movie studio, a publishing company, or a television news station?

**ARE YOU CURIOUS ABOUT** what actors, bloggers, graphic designers, museum curators, or writers do?

 ## Business & Administration

**WOULD YOU ENJOY** playing Monopoly, being the boss of your favorite club or team, or starting your own business?

**CAN YOU IMAGINE** someday working at a big corporate headquarters, government agency, or international business center?

**ARE YOU CURIOUS ABOUT** what brand managers, chief executive officers, e-commerce analysts, entrepreneurs, or purchasing agents do?

 ## Education & Training

**WOULD YOU ENJOY** babysitting, teaching your grandparents how to use a computer, or running a summer camp for neighbor kids in your backyard?

**CAN YOU IMAGINE** someday working at a college counseling center, corporate training center, or school?

**ARE YOU CURIOUS ABOUT** what animal trainers, coaches, college professors, guidance counselors, or principals do?

##  Finance

**WOULD YOU ENJOY** earning and saving money, being the class treasurer, or playing the stock market game?

**CAN YOU IMAGINE** someday working at an accounting firm, bank, or Wall Street stock exchange?

**ARE YOU CURIOUS ABOUT** what accountants, bankers, fraud investigators, property managers, or stockbrokers do?

##  Food & Natural Resources

**WOULD YOU ENJOY** exploring nature, growing your own garden, or setting up a recycling center at your school?

**CAN YOU IMAGINE** someday working at a national park, raising crops in a city farm, or studying food in a laboratory?

**ARE YOU CURIOUS ABOUT** what landscape architects, chefs, food scientists, environmental engineers, or forest rangers do?

## Government

**WOULD YOU ENJOY** reading about U.S. presidents, running for student council, or helping a favorite candidate win an election?

**CAN YOU IMAGINE** someday working at a chamber of commerce, government agency, or law firm?

**ARE YOU CURIOUS** about what mayors, customs agents, federal special agents, intelligence analysts, or politicians do?

##  Health Sciences

**WOULD YOU ENJOY** nursing a sick pet back to health, dissecting animals in a science lab, or helping the school coach run a sports clinic?

**CAN YOU IMAGINE** someday working at a dental office, hospital, or veterinary clinic?

**ARE YOU CURIOUS ABOUT** what art therapists, doctors, dentists, pharmacists, and veterinarians do?

##  Hospitality & Tourism

**WOULD YOU ENJOY** traveling, sightseeing, or meeting people from other countries?

**CAN YOU IMAGINE** someday working at a convention center, resort, or travel agency?

**ARE YOU CURIOUS ABOUT** what convention planners, golf pros, tour guides, resort managers, or wedding planners do?

## Human Services

**WOULD YOU ENJOY** showing a new kid around your school, organizing a neighborhood food drive, or being a peer mediator?

**CAN YOU IMAGINE** someday working at an elder care center, fitness center, or mental health center?

**ARE YOU CURIOUS ABOUT** what elder care center directors, hairstylists, personal trainers, psychologists, or religious leaders do?

## Information Technology

**WOULD YOU ENJOY** creating your own video game, setting up a Web site, or building your own computer?

**CAN YOU IMAGINE** someday working at an information technology start-up company, software design firm, or research and development laboratory?

**ARE YOU CURIOUS ABOUT** what artificial intelligence scientists, big data analysts, computer forensic investigators, software engineers, or video game designers do?

## Law & Public Safety

**WOULD YOU ENJOY** working on the school safety patrol, participating in a mock court trial at school, or coming up with a fire escape plan for your home?

**CAN YOU IMAGINE** someday working at a cyber security company, fire station, police department, or prison?

**ARE YOU CURIOUS ABOUT** what animal control officers, coroners, detectives, firefighters, or park rangers do?

 ## Marketing

**WOULD YOU ENJOY** keeping up with the latest fashion trends, picking favorite TV commercials during Super Bowl games, or making posters for a favorite school club?

**CAN YOU IMAGINE** someday working at an advertising agency, corporate marketing department, or retail store?

**ARE YOU CURIOUS ABOUT** what creative directors, market researchers, media buyers, retail store managers, and social media consultants do?

 ## Science, Technology, Engineering & Mathematics (STEM)

**WOULD YOU ENJOY** concocting experiments in a science lab, trying out the latest smartphone, or taking advanced math classes?

**CAN YOU IMAGINE** someday working in a science laboratory, engineering firm, or research and development center?

**ARE YOU CURIOUS ABOUT** what aeronautical engineers, ecologists, statisticians, oceanographers, or zoologists do?

## Transportation

**WOULD YOU ENJOY** taking pilot or sailing lessons, watching a NASA rocket launch, or helping out in the school carpool lane?

**CAN YOU IMAGINE** someday working at an airport, mass transit system, or shipping port?

**ARE YOU CURIOUS ABOUT** what air traffic controllers, flight attendants, logistics planners, surveyors, and traffic engineers do?

# MY WoW

## I am here.

Name

Grade

School

## Who I am.

Make a word collage! Use 5 adjectives to form a picture that describes who you are.

## Where I'm going.

The next career pathway I want to explore is

Some things I need to learn first to succeed.

1

2

3

My Career Choice

## To get here.

# GLOSSARY

**airframe and powerplant (A&P) technician**
person who is a certified aviation mechanic

**automate**
to run or operate a factory or system by using machines, computers, and robots instead of people to do the work

**computer-aided manufacturing (CAM) programmer**
person who uses computer software to control machines and tools used in the manufacturing process

**electrical engineer**
person who uses the technology of electricity to work on a wide range of components, devices, and systems

**environmental solutions director**
person who oversees the environmental strategies, policies, and programs of a company

**fuselage**
the main body of an aircraft where the passengers, crew, and cargo are carried

**hangars**
large buildings where airplanes are kept and repaired

**industrial designer**
person who designs products, tools, packaging, and other resources used in manufacturing

**manufacturing**
all the jobs involved in making products on a large scale using special equipment or machinery

**nanometers**
units of length in the metric system; one nanometer is equal to one-billionth of a meter

**nanotechnologist**
scientist who works with materials on an atomic or molecular scale

**nanotechnology**
technology that attempts to harness extremely small things such as atoms and molecules

**portfolio**
a set of drawings kept in a folder that show someone's skills to a potential employer

**production manager**
person who plans, coordinates, and controls manufacturing processes

**robotics**
the science of designing, making, and using robots

**robotics engineer**
person who creates robots that are able to perform duties that humans either are unable or prefer not to complete

**sustainable**
done in a way that can be continued and doesn't use up natural resources

# INDEX

**\* Refers to the Web page sources**

## About the Author

Diane Lindsey Reeves is the author of lots of children's books. She has written several original PEANUTS stories (published by Regnery Kids and Sourcebooks). She is especially curious about what people do and likes to write books that get kids thinking about all the cool things they can be when they grow up. She lives in Cary, North Carolina, and her favorite thing to do is play with her grandkids—Conrad, Evan, Reid, and Hollis Grace.